The Miracle of Mercury

poems by

Joan Hanna

Finishing Line Press
Georgetown, Kentucky

The Miracle of Mercury

Copyright © 2016 by Joan Hanna
ISBN 978-1-944251-37-6 First Edition
All rights reserved under International and Pan-American Copyright Conventions.
No part of this book may be reproduced in any manner whatsoever without written permission from the publisher, except in the case of brief quotations embodied in critical articles and reviews.

Editor: Christen Kincaid

Cover Image: Metal Splashing, Ripples and Waves - Sutterstock.com

Author Photo: Craig Elliott Hanna

Cover Design: Joan Hanna

Printed in the USA on acid-free paper.
Order online: www.finishinglinepress.com
    also available on amazon.com

> Author inquiries and mail orders:
> Finishing Line Press
> P. O. Box 1626
> Georgetown, Kentucky 40324
> U. S. A.

Table of Contents

Mercury 1

Thirteen 6

"Wish You Were Here" 8

Before The Rubber and Needle 11

Bobby 12

Tile and Stone 13

Rick 17

Copper 19

Sometimes 22

Skip 23

Death Mask 25

Glass 26

*To all of the ghosts lingering on these pages:
You touched my soul, wounded my heart and nurtured my eternal sorrow.
You are my chronicle, my melancholy and my sheltered layers of truth
in all of its imperfection.*

*To Craig:
How you continue to believe in me when I keep falling into these chasms
will always bewilder and amaze me. You, my lovely husband,
have the courage of ten lions.*

Mercury

I

The first time I touched mercury
it lay on the linoleum of my
grandmother's kitchen. Someone

(probably me) had dropped a glass
thermometer and scattered shimmering
silver balls across the floor. I nudged

and pushed them into one another
each glob swallowed up the other
colliding at my fingertips until

one slightly lopsided circle sat
in the middle of glass shards from
the shattered thermometer. I didn't

care about the glass. Didn't care
that it slid into the skin of my finger-
tips. Didn't care that the glass

distorted the mercury with a
dissimilar icy shininess. I just
wanted to dink my finger into

the middle and watch the mercury
explode into pieces so I could
move them along and into each

other; over and over again. I was
about five or six. And already
saw the world this way: out of

the broken came the fascinating.
Out of the shattered came new
dimensions. My mother (or

grandmother) caught me
and began to shush me out
of the way with warnings of

*watch the broken glass and
you'll cut yourself and don't
touch the mercury it will burn

you.* I tried to show them how
the mercury moved. How it was
solid and liquid and metal all at

the same time. How it challenged
fingertips and cherrywood floor.
How it gathered up the glass, specks

of dust and dirt and still shined.
Still shimmered. Still wobbled. Even as
it was scooped up and tossed out

with admonitions about *carelessness*,
clumsiness and *danger.* Always
the pointing to *danger.* Always the

abortion of allure. The second time
I touched mercury was on purpose. I took
the thermometer into the bathroom. Settled

onto the floor and tried to snap it cleanly
in half. I wanted to separate the glass from
the mercury and have it pour out all on its

own. I wanted this shimmery, reflective
solid-liquid all to myself without the
scares. Without the danger cries. Without

diluting my pristine fascination. Without
anything taken from the experience
of mercury moving at my tiny fingertips.

II

The first time I saw the evidence
green chunks of glass were everywhere;

nestled into the gullies of the porcelain
sink top, caught between the black cast

iron legs of stove grates; sprayed
across the counters and table mingling

with the cigarette butts dotted
along the floor and tumbled with

the larger chunks of the shattered
ashtray that seemed to litter

everything in the kitchen including
my little brother's high chair. The floor

crunched and squished under our
sneakered feet as we padded into the

aftermath of the wreckage in the kitchen.
Waking to the commotion and imagining

how the sounds fit together was
one thing; seeing this evidence was

another. My mother was sniffling
as she tried to sweep the floor. HE

had left the house. I don't know
what my brothers were doing but I

fascinated myself with the tiny
orbs of glass against the black

cast iron; how they caught
the overhead light; how the

edges were smoothed and jagged
all at once. But then the babies

were crying and I was herded
back up into my room to wonder

about crashing broken glass and tangles
of angry voices that wake children

in the middle of the night. The
first time I saw the evidence

was like walking into a storm-
ravaged shed after the wind ripped

everything apart. You step slowly
and lightly around the damage

so you don't disturb unsettled
energy and begin the hurling again.

III

The second time I saw the evidence, I
expected it. I had learned many things
from the crashing of green shattered
glass. Learned when to stay under covers.
When to peek through the spokes of wooden
railings while sitting in a ball silently

at the top of stairs. Holding my breath until
the door slammed and the only sounds
were random sniffling and a dull scratching
of glass moving on linoleum. It was then
that I could safely crawl back into bed. Pull
the covers up and cry into my pillow.
It was too soon that I realized that not
all shattered glass held the miracle
of mercury moving at your fingertips.

Thirteen

I

The pond water trembled as if heaving
with the coupling of dragonflies. These
concussive circles: two, two and
two pulsing ripples moving like
impulse-dampened daydreams,
recalling an undulating water-like
birth of sorts in a roughly uncontrolled
pausing. Waiting. Pausing; as if some
familiar sequence was ready to begin.

II

I can almost feel that first gasp. That
first punch in the chest as air filled
into a constricted place where stillness
had been. The reaching and clasping
for illusive air; the blemished clashing
of loud, clattering voices. I reach back
and back as if this clue could help me
understand why this chest tightness
remains. This hollow calling out into
an empty room. This vague attempt
to clutch; to clench; to breathe.

III

These photographs of yours haunt me. They
muddle about me as if they should be my
memories too. But these are the innocuous,
innocent preservations of your *outdoor* face.
Your—*neighbors are watching* face. Your—
50s Ladies Home Journal pearls and pumps
public persona face. That ridiculous Gimbel's
postcard in our appropriate Norman Rockwell
Christmas garb, which you really believed
was true. Your revision of history stares back
at me like mocking embarrassments igniting
the hot, liquid poison of that first gasp of air
breathed into my already brittle spine.

IV

You hovered above me in a medusa rage.
My feet tangled around spindled chair legs;
head tucked into thin, pubescent arms that
swathed my face; my eyes. My back, spine,
and shoulder bearing the burden of you.
Ears ringing with that mechanism that
takes us up and out of ourselves like
some anesthesia of the soul until
there is only the rug under polished toes;
the curved seat of a hard, unyielding solid
wood; your voice somewhere outside of me
saying something I cannot bear to hear.

"Wish You Were Here"
(Pink Floyd)

Like when I was sitting
At your kitchen table in
           Fairview,
With the floor boards
Vibrating frames off the
           Walls,
As the thump from amps
Pounded into my growing
           Infatuation
With the bass player for
No apparent reason.
           Wandering
Over aimlessly during
Band practice while your
           Babies
Slept upstairs and the
Band rehearsed in the
           Basement.
You, folding diapers and
Tiny socks while I tried to
           Bleed
Into a new world and
Escape everything. The
           Pot
Smooth and wafting into
My lungs. You, leaving the
           House
Grinning, that grin you
Always had when you were
           High.

Leaving me alone with
My obsession. The sheer
          Terror
Of it striking me some-
Where deep in my coiled
          Gut,
Rumbling and churning
Until I panicked and
          Puked
For an hour in your bath-
Room because the pot, or
          Paranoia
Or the fear of something
New, or old or maybe the
          Same
Old *see ya later, sister*
Casualness was more
          Than
I could hold in the
Palm of my ineffective
          Hand.
Was it a counterfeit
Alligator tye-dyed clip
          Strap
That sent me rushing into
It; imagining I was free?
          God,
Even my hash pipe
Went to Woodstock
          Instead

Of me; I slithered
Into obscure empty
          Galaxies
Of the *uncool* scratching
At my enflamed hash-
          Hives.
Embarrassed because I
Puked up pot like a
          Teenager
Burning at the throat of
The first taste of Vodka
          Freedom
Only to slide two fingers
Down into the back of her
          Tongue
To stop the room from
Spinning; or, the people
          Leaving;
Or, the incessant high
Increasing the raging
          Paranoia
Or insatiable need to
Wish someone were
          Here.

Before The Rubber And Needle

giveaways, before the closing
of the bath houses, Before the
cocktail, Gatsby's was faux 30s
deco walls and Sundays of salvaged
French-ruffled couches tucked behind
curtain shadowed corners. At seven,
a disembodied voice oozed "The boo-fay
is now open" breaking the beat of early
80s techno-remixes of 70s dance tunes.
When I couldn't breath through
the cloud of mingled smoke, amyl poppers
and sweat intensified Lagerfeld, I
escaped to the upstairs lounge
swapping out white wine for
Perrier with a twist. Talking to
pretty-boys who tolerated just
another fag-hag hiding behind
hetero security and a bull dyke
writing lesbian love poems to me
while laying silken folk vocals
over a hesitant guitar pretending
I could be her lipstick other half, if only
I would just give in and come out. But
I was camouflaging freshly sliced
divorce lesions and hiding from myself.
We were all playing these homo-hetero
hiding games, until the pretty-boys started
dying and everyone was HIV scared sick.
When it was one too many 24-hour
mandatory crematoriums and one
too many close-to-home calls,
I so unfairly slipped casually back
into my own world, escaping
the perceived terror of death
in every innocent off-hand kiss.

Bobby

In the day room of Ancora Mental Hospital
Bobby pretended he was getting well again.
Glancing sideways to the clock, waiting
for an out of place click, still hearing
electronic chirps and whirs, *and
not just in my head*, he murmured to the clock,
to the phone, to the intercom, to the wall *like
the doctors kept insisting*. He wanted to cross
the room, crush the courtesy phone into fractured
plastic and twisted wires like his phones at home.
But he knew they were watching. Bobby wanted
to gut everything in his brain, wanted to pull all things
out of his mind, wanted to unbolt his head, unhinge his
jaw and pour in enough drugs to slaughter the
paranoia. It was easy to pretend he was better, playing
Crazy Eights on a sunny afternoon, ignoring
the shouts and screams coming through
the third floor men's lock down. *Just seven days
to get straight and sober?* He smiled knowing
it was not enough time to forget
the voices. Forget the newly implanted
microchip. Forget they were still listening.
Seven days for all of us to pretend it was drugs
and not a psychotic break so we could feel
safe. Seven days of Bobby looking at other inmates
like we had looked at him the night he washed his life
of radios, cameras and microphones. Just when
sanity seemed to crest the horizon he asked *Do they
jam frequencies in this hospital? Cause I can't hear
them anymore.* Just seven short days of silence
before he went home and *they* would again listen
to every word he spoke, whispered or thought;
even the deep breathing he couldn't consciously
control in his sleep. *And, I know they are still out there.*
He tapped his temple. *And, that's why they never get me.*

Tile And Stone

I

Somewhere in a box tucked under the eaves
of our crawlspace, wrapped in old, yellowing
newspaper are small rocks. Pebbles. Bits of
discarded glass, shell and wood I collect
to punctuate moments passed. These
fragments of earth and stone remind me
how low I've been; how far I've come or
where my roots lay tangled far into the past.
Some roots are intertwined with my permission
but many are not. I stumble upon these apparitions
haphazardly while unpacking or organizing
and am always surprised by the wash of
reminiscence. It is as if I have passed all emotion
into these inanimate objects for safekeeping.

II

The broken corner of blue tile from a crumbling
house in Italy where my grandmother was born is
all I have of her life there and although it seems
trivial, it is the farthest I can trace my coil of roots
back to their beginnings. The picture of this house
meant nothing to me. It's corroded shutters and crumbling
foundation only seemed to set firm this idea of
impermanence and the fragility of things left behind. But
to hold this tiny piece of tile in my hand was to touch
the clay and earth beneath my grandmother's feet. It was
to feel coupled to where I originated. It was tactile and real.
A piece of the house, once a part of her, now sits in my hand.
It becomes a part of me. And when I hold, this broken bit

of sun-baked homeland in my palm, it gives me warmth
and a kind of satisfaction as if I had been the one to travel
by plane, train and car to pluck it from the rubble of
her birthplace. It sits in my palm warm and satisfying
as if it were a piece to an unknown mystery finally
found. This small chunk of tile brings solidity
to a place, which only existed in my grandmother's
memory of whispered stories long forgotten now
by her grandchildren. It references a place
I will never know but somehow always remember.

III

It is now the lifting fog of a haunting sunrise dream
as I cried out to leafless, branches hanging over an
empty grey sky and ducks paddling at a shallow,
lapping not yet frozen water's edge. My voice splitting
silence in this lost, hibernated scene of rushing air
and creak and groan of winter branches. Each morning,
pulling myself out of a warm bed, shrugging into layers
and walking to this spot on this bench; so the cold could
penetrate petrified skin and sinew. Coming here to escape
the palipitatious banging of my heart in my ears; against
my chest. Coming here to see something new, to hear
something new. This was where I came to speak to God.
The Creator. The Goddess. The Universe. To ask: why?
To ask: why not? To ask: When? Where? How long and
how much further? I came to watch the lake's water rush
and thrash beneath a frozen surface. I came to feel warm
blood pumping through a dulled heart diminished by anger,
doubt and fear. This was my exercise in survival. This was
the place where I met myself mirrored in the deep frozen

lake. My Narcissus turning away from a gaunt reflection. Bare branches bent to their limits. A wind that entered deep into apathetic bone and marrow. Left behind like the ducks paddling and sliding, searching for a foothold, awaiting the warmth of sun and companionship. The creak of ice and limb became the crack of a thawing, retreating winter. The snowed ground was soon specked with relentless crocus and stubborn fescue. Shivering, slipping ducks now waddling mothers and fluffed up baby chicks paddling furiously behind their expanded group. Trails in front of the bench filled with joggers and overhead branches flushed into canopies shading the sun. I had been sitting on that bench for months—asking the same questions every day: why? Why not? Where? When? How long? How much further?

IV

My only answer was spring. When finally even the earliest of days filled the trail with walkers, joggers and children running through the paths. I had lost my frozen confessional. And on the last day of my self-condemning exile I reached down to the ground beneath this companion bench and grasped a small, brown, uneven stone. I cradled it in my palm and closed a fist around it until my fingers were numb; shifting the memory of this place; the stillness, the loneliness, the creak of limb, the crash of wind, the rush of partially frozen water, which had punctuated my shouts to the sky. I pushed my shame into this tiny stone warming the center of my palm. My memoir filled this stone with a notion of almost possible resolution. As I walked away from that bench where I had faced the collapse of my life, I no longer saw bare trees and frozen lake. But knew,

as I felt this stone in my hand, I had looked into the face
of my own and not Dante's descent. Not the flame but the
cold chill of the lost standing at the bitter edge
of a road without a crossroad to choose.

V

This was all the truth I knew: the clattering determination
of a solitary woman holding onto tree and water and sky
because all others had faded away. This was the bench
and the tiny rock that reminded me that I can. I will.
I have survived. As I walked down the path away from
the bench, tracing the ridges and the shift from smooth
indent to rough edge of this small foothold in my hand,
I put that winter behind me and placed the memory of it
all within that tiny compression of earth. In my mind this
stone and blue tile unite and become roots entangled
into one another—a tile from where I began and a rock
punctuating where I now begin again. A newly forged
circle somehow completed. Somewhere in the basement
of a new life, in old, yellowing newspaper, folded into
boxes, stacked under eaves, in a quiet crawlspace, a small
blue tile from the house my grandmother was born and
a rock from a bench by a frozen lake hold the unspoken
fracture of connective branches leading back to me.

Rick

Dancing through clothes racks
speed tics synthesized
into a Jagger impression,
blond shagged hair
falling onto the shoulders of a
Warhol pop art velvet jacket.
He could have been a rock star,
talk show host
or head shop owner
instead of a Vietnam vet
junkie cliché. I stocked shelves,
put out hash pipes,
bongs and rolling papers. Pressed
gigantic keys on an antique
gold filigree cash register, pushing money
into a drawer that would never
make it to the bank.
Rick left me to watch the store
when he crashed, taking money
from the register and driving into Camden
to the doctor monitoring his methadone
with extra doses and side 'scrips
of meth and coke. He'd come back
energized, carting steaming cups of coffee,
cartons of cigarettes and sugary
cakes and donuts. Paying
my afternoon work with
jeans, tees, handmade belts
and Indian jewelry
before clicking through a beaded curtain
to spend the rest of the day high

in the back room.
He talked about 'Nam only once,
about an old man
who served tea in a dirty shop in Saigon.
The only place he felt safe
"over there" until he found the soothing drugs
he said, saved his life. He smuggled
a rifle into the states
his only souvenir, except for
the nightmares and increasing
insomnia. When the methadone,
the meth and the coke
no longer shut out the war;
when the money ran out
and the words of an old man
faded away the only thing
he had left was the gun, slid
into his mouth and one last pull
on a trigger; one last click.

Copper

I

The first time I tasted metal, the blood
slid from behind my nose and onto
the back of my tongue tasting like wet
copper pennies and wine left out
in the sun too long. I was watching
the red droplets fall like dotted beads
onto the book in my lap. Everything
was this taste of fermented
bitter copper and the dewdrops
on the homework sheet and the
absorption into the book. I didn't
listen to my mother's shouting and
screaming. I didn't care about her.
I ignored her by staring at how the
drops hit and seemed to try to
escape by bouncing up and
expanding as if they were reaching
for something to grab onto only to be
towed back onto the page where
they splattered into oddly shaped
distortions that crept out and
expanded into the paper below.

II

I knew I would get throttled with a ruler
by one of the nuns tomorrow. That
was why I was crying; it wasn't the wet
gobs of tears that had smeared
my math homework. It wasn't that
my mother had surprised-slapped me
so hard that my eight-year-old neck
snapped back as blood slid and bubbled
into my throat. It was the threat of that
goddamned ruler that I wasn't going to
escape when they saw the damaged book.
That is what terrified me. And I would take it.
I would take the *Jesus is so disappointed
in you* lecture. I would stand in front
of the class and bow my head in the
expected posture for the *look at this
slothful, disrespectful child bent on
going to hell* allocution. Look remorseful
when told that *Jesus took the nails for me
and I was such an ungrateful sinner*. Stare
down at my feet for the *look upon her and learn
to fear God* homily. I would still taste the metal
biting into my lip, trying not to cry. Would
feel these copper-basted shards of glass edge
into my defiant sinner's heart begging for the
fires of hell to engulf me in a sudden euphoric
flame like my heretic-branded patron saint.

III

The last time I tasted metal at their hand,
I was trapped between them trying to
extract or detract or some other deluded
thought of escape when the intended back-
hand swing caught me full on the mouth. Teeth
jolted together with an off-kilter bang. The
disorienting snap. The immediate swell.
The bruised tingle. The rush of copper
sliding along crooked teeth. They made
comical exaggerated gestures on the lawn
like tiny stick figure replicas of themselves
shouting for me; at me; about me; at each
other. I had once again tasted the metal of
my own blood. I pushed my feet to make it to
the corner; to turn the corner; to keep moving.
All my concentration on dragging sideways
on a cigarette burning through my hamburgered
lip. It was too late—the miracle of mercury was
already enslaved within this taste of bitter copper.

Sometimes

who we've been
melts
into a limbo
we can't control
and we sit
mesmerized
by the energy
of time passing

Skip

Skip considered himself a connoisseur
taking drugs seasonally like
a fashion accessory;
Heroin for slow, cold winter nights,
speed for longer, brighter days
of summer.
Heroin slowed him, gave him
artistic inspiration and days
shut into himself.
Speed made him a socially
energized host filled with rants and
cravings for chocolate-covered Tastycakes
and can after can after can of
Tab diet soda.
He lived in an unfurnished back room
with a flat mattress, the clothes on his back
and some art supplies
in a wrinkled brown paper bag.
I stole food
from my mother's kitchen, tucked
a note in between a liverwurst sandwich and
Butterscotch Krimpets and left the bag
on my way to school.
I fluttered on the edges
of a teenage George Harrison crush,
Skip's long hair and beard obscuring
everything, except for those
flashes of wild dark eyes. He took me
to an Allman Brothers concert for my
18th birthday, on the ride home
kissed me softly and said,
"don't ever walk into a room

with a closed door."
One day three guys lifted him,
cursing, fighting, kicking
and dumped him into a tub.
"Third time this week"
one of them said and turned on the shower.
Ice-cold water hit him, forcing his clothes
into the bones of his back,
shoulders and legs,
matting the long hair and beard
against his hollowed cheekbones.
Soaking him
until the artist, the story teller,
the crush drained from me
and his eyes,
his heroin crazy, Charlie Manson eyes,
stared blankly as if
he didn't even remember my name.

Death Mask

Your skin pulled taut across
your jawbone, your cheekbones.
Sharp, hollow ridges hugged tightly
by alabaster skin, clinging
to the face that once was you.

Your skin pulls at every bump,
curve and ridge. Hands
curled into balls, lying on your bony chest
moving up. Down. Up. Down
to the rhythm of your breathing.

I sit beside you for days
and count down the final breaths
of your life. Matching your breathing
with my own. Counting,
because there is nothing left to do.
Counting, hoping you will continue
to breathe, knowing you will not.

A short pause holds us suspended
and I hold my breath as your lips
contort with one long escaping
hush of air, until there is only
rigid skin clinging to bone.

Glass

I had ducked just in time to watch
the porcelain ashtray dent the wall, litter
everything with discarded ash and cigarettes

and drop into big, unflattering chunks around
my bare feet. I didn't see the pattern yet; didn't
know that shattered glass follows you everywhere

like little annoying slivers that slide in through
your fingertips nestle into your thumbs and palms
like entrenched organisms that accumulate.

Build. Congregate. Eventually even slide into
the edges of protected cores; crystalizing
into rigid pinpoints of contradiction that let you

see only right in front of you; and nothing of
the forewarning. I knew I pushed buttons. Did it
on purpose. It was my only security; my only

obtainable voice. So I waited for the opening and
struck. Swiftly. Then, the drop; the closing of eyes;
the clenching of teeth; the wait. Why the hell was it

always these big, clunky lead-crystal things that thudded
and crumbled leaving fragments in corners, under
stoves and refrigerators. These reminders that popped

up or out or tumbled into the center of the room so you
step on them for months. Always the treading on shattered
glass; always these obtrusive edges glaring at you.

Always the crash. The forfeiture. The resultant
embryonic quiet. When I recognized this crystalline
pattern of repetition; of regeneration I told myself

The Lie. But when I challenged the initial shadow
of the truth it was as spellbinding as mercury.
As sharp as exhausted glass; as bitter as the bite of copper

on the teeth. Then it was all me. It was shooting imbedded
shards of glass out of my fingertips and spitting chunks
of undigested blood-soaked mercury and ash out of my

mouth like some banshee vomiting over-indulged
denial. It was a cleansing. A spew of deep, empowering
consummation. It expended all of my rage. Released

every fear. Cut every connection. I was too intoxicated
by once again feeling the miracle of mercury moving
at my fingertips to even comprehend the depth of this

unrelenting chasm that opened up before me. Instead
I relished the small sobbing mass he slid into on the
floor with a slight flex of my upper lip. A small yet

satisfying curl of involuntary bliss. I walked away
ignoring the metal tang itching on the edges of broken
glass that slid quietly in through the soles of my feet.

Joan Hanna was born and raised in Philadelphia and now lives in New Jersey with her husband, Craig and her insomnia, which she has decided to name George.

She writes poetry, nonfiction, and fiction and also spins a pretty nice review. She likes to ask tough questions in interviews, which she is convinced is going to turn back around on her one of these days.

In her spare time and when not obsessing about her own writing, Hanna is all about reading, reading, reading, music, movies and binge watching TV shows. I think this might be the George talking.

Her debut chapbook, *Threads*, was published in 2013 by Finishing Line Press and was also named a Finalist in the 2014 Next Generation Indie Book Awards.

Projects currently feeding the George:

Hanna's three-part essay: Place in Poetry: Concussive Reverberations appeared on TheThepoetry Blog in October 2014 and her essay, *Untangling the Roots*, on her relationship with language, appeared in the *Poets' Quarterly* summer issue in 2014.

Hanna is seeking representation for a Science Fiction novel, currently titled: *Are You Still My Girl?*

Her nonfiction story, *Breathing*, appeared in the Shorts on

Survival section in the October 2010 issue of *r.kv.r.y*. Hanna is currently looking for a publisher for a nonfiction story collection, which includes this story.

Hanna's book reviews and interviews have appeared at *r.kv.r.y. Quarterly Literary Journal*, The Ashland University MFA Blog, *Poets' Quarterly* and *Examiner.com*. She also writes book reviews for Author Exposure because it's a great place to showcase new and emerging writers.

Other Editorial passions include: Assistant Editor, Nonfiction/Poetry for r.*kv.r.y. Quarterly Literary Journa*l; Assistant Managing Editor of *River Teeth, A Journal of Nonfiction Narrative*; Senior Editor for *Glassworks Magazine*, published by Rowan University. She is also the former Managing Editor and sometimes contributor for *Poets' Quarterly*.

Hanna holds an MFA in Creative Writing in Poetry and Nonfiction from Ashland University and teaches creative writing at Rowan University. Follow Hanna (and the adventures of George) at her personal blog: www.writingthroughquicksand.blogspot.com.

www.ingramcontent.com/pod-product-compliance
Lightning Source LLC
Chambersburg PA
CBHW060225050426
42446CB00013B/3178